Up Close and Personal:
The Poems and Photographs of
Arnold David Richards

Up Close and Personal:
The Poems and Photographs
of Arnold David Richards

Arnold David Richards

IPBOOKS.net
International Psychoanalytic Books

International Psychoanalytic Books

New York • http://www.IPBooks.net

Published by IPBooks, Queens, NY
Online at IPBooks.net

All Photographs by the author.

Cover layout by Kathy Kovacic, Blackthorn Studio.
Cover Painting: El Lissitzky, *Untitled*, 1920.
Interior design and layout by Noel S. Morado

ISBN: 978-1-956864-75-5

Foreword

DR. RICHARDS has given this collection the perfect title, for they are indeed "up close and personal. Although a renowned psychoanalyst, he is not "full of himself," as the kids would say. Narcissism is not in the least part of his character. What we see in these wise, memoir-like and spiritual poems is a humble Brooklyn boy, grown older and deeply aware of his own and our impending deaths. Eros must yield, he reminds us all, to Thanatos.

Like any reader, I have my favorites. The very first is "Boss: A Hasidic Parable," which he perhaps ought to consider placing at the beginning of the book. Next is "Elegy for Muriel," which tightly conveys the personality of its subject. Then, "Boro Park," for the humility of the repeated phrase "if you don't mind."

The same humility is apparent in "Brighton Private," of course. And finally, "Scissors and Paste," where he nails it down for us, in case we had any doubts.

So, dear friends, open, begin to read and savor these pages.

—Irene Willis
Poetry Editor, IPBooks

Contents

Boss: A Meditation

A Hasidic Parable

When the great Rabbi Israel Baal Shem-Tov saw misfortune threatening the Jews it was his custom to go into a certain part of the forest to meditate. There he would light a fire, say a special prayer, and the miracle would be accomplished and the misfortune averted.

Later, when his disciple, the celebrated Magid of Mezritch, had occasion, for the same reason, to intercede with heaven, he would go to the same place in the forest and say: "Master of the Universe, listen! I do not know how to light the fire, but I am still able to say the prayer," and again the miracle would be accomplished.

Still later, Rabbi Moshe-Leib of Sasov, in order to save his people once more, would go into the forest and say: "I do not know how to light the fire, I do not know the prayer, but I know the place and this must be sufficient." It was sufficient and the miracle was accomplished.

Then it fell to Rabbi Israel of Rizhyn to overcome misfortune. Sitting in his armchair, his head in his hands, he spoke to God: "I am unable to light the fire and I do not know the prayer; I cannot even find the place in the forest. All I can do is to tell the story, and this must be sufficient." And it was sufficient.

God made man because he loves stories.
— Elie Wiesel, *The Gates of the Forest*

The largest structure in the universe
838 separate galaxies
One billion light years across
Four connected clusters
How many moons planets?
People like us
We start the day
Infinite worlds
Inconceivable
All the concerns of our
Life seem reasonable
We think
Boss laughs
Inconsequential
And us
Infinitesimal

Arlene

you are my wife
and you are my life
you are my love
you are my treasure
the fount of my pleasure
you connect
with the depth of my being
life worth living
beginning without ending
always connected
and connecting
we are a double helix
intertwined
you and me
you grace the hours
and all our days

Friends

friends for ever and ever

always for the better

caring and sharing

a life time of memories

indelible

now and then

and always

Father's Day

My father had a stubble beard
a crippled gait, a sad face, a quiet voice

My father had a troubled life.
Mother died before her time.
Brother struck by Cossack blade.
Father carried the body home.
Sister shot in dark ravine.
A world destroyed, A god that failed..

My father grew old. His hair turned white.
A wrinkled suit wrapped his frame,

He walked home.
Stooped, returned to wife
Bandit waited in darkened hall

Blood unstopped stained the wall.

My father had a troubled life,
a crippled gait, a stubble beard
a sad face, a quiet voice

A troubled life
And then he died.

Mother's Day

My mother was
a Hallmark junkie.
Collected cards
Dates received
recorded in her book
pages wide-ruled
black-and-white
speckled cover
the gift noted
where applicable
House plant:
"It lasts but it needs
watering"
Flowers by telegraph:
"A visit would
have been better"
A thimble to add
to her collection.

She hung the cards
on a line strung
across the rough stone
basement wall
white powdered surface
sheets out to dry
printed wishes
flower-bordered
rhymed couplets
written by
the poet laureates
of Kansas City.

Petersburg, VA, 1965

I was the jailer
You were the jailed

We plotted your escape.
Dark night at Southern Depot.
First stop on the underground railway
Route to freedom.

No more chain gang dogs Greyhound
route to freedom.

Missed by a minute or less
Sinking heart, sweaty palms
Who decided you or I Impala
Route to freedom

No more nigger work wife I 95
Route to freedom.

For My Much Younger Sister on the Occasion of Her Birthday

Shall I mark your birthday when you did not mark mine?

We both started in same space but at the wrong time.
I too soon. You too late.
You Sara's gift.. I a mistake

Down the same canal. Greeted by the same face
Brought to the same place.
Crowded and cluttered rooms with little view.
Windows covered with damask opaque to leaves and sky
Furniture covered with plastic.
Transparent in pattern shielding texture from the feel of
sticky fingers
yours and mine.

We both ate In the same kitchen. Sanitas on the walls,
linoleum on the floor
Fox Ubet Chocolate MyT Fine

We shared space and place faced but not time.
I came to love the man who also made us both.
You were taught otherwise.

Who cut our ties of birth?
I am our father's son.
You are our mother's child.

A Wreath of Verses
(On the Fresh Grave of Toni
Greenberg)

Color it black
If you don' t mind
Her eyes shut tight
"Shakhor b'eynayim"
Black decorates our hall
Our no longer happy
Birthday Party and hers
Danzig/Vilna 1925
God would not delay
Her departure for our
Benefit

Color it black
Color of mourning
Darkens our vision
"Tunkl in di oygn"
She carried history

On her person
Khasidik Queen
Superordinate to Kaiser
And Emperor
God would not delay
Her departure for our
Purpose

Color it black
If you don't mind
Her eyes shut tight
"Khoyshekh b'eynayim"
Curtain falls
On Central Park window
Dusk drops early in December
But it was a warm autumn
Did God delay winter
This year to ease her exit?

Color it black
Funereal
Yankele, Toni's emissary
And God's messenger

Followed her instructions
To the letter
Stamped with date/time

Like a computer
She summoned the players
For the final performance
She was a star .
She had the right
To schedule closing night
For her benefit
"Finster in di oygn"
Color it darkness

Elegy for Muriel

You celebrated your self
and rightly so.
You reveled in your senses,
pampered them with aliment
sonatas and sauces
flavorful.
You tuned your body
Sharpened its sensuality
prepared for its adornment,
clothes your advertisement.
You wrote your own
jacket copy
prideful
before your
fall.

Muriel Weinstein, PhD died two summers ago. She fell off
a mountain in Switzerland where she loved to climb

Boro Park

Color it red
If you don't mind
I will call
a spade a spade
was it a buck knife
or switch blade impaled the painter' s chest wall
red blood spurting
on tiled floor
of dark hallway
headline in The Forward
CRIPPLE STABBED IN BORO PARK
red blood like spray paint
my father's last job
price complete
includes labor and materials,

He always lived dangerously
soldier-librarian
in Trotsky's army

he escaped bandits
and commissars
British shells
crashing on Odessa
Romanian border guards
Arabs In Galilee
He came to America
land of promise
He died the day after
the Fourth of July
red white and blue
celebration of
our revolution
ironic, ex-Bolshevik
killed by worker
dead like brother
bayoneted by Pitlura

He should have stuck to books
or stayed
a worker, Mottle
the boss not the
operator. Or kept

the payroll In the bank,
skipped the evening news
and advertised in the
Yellow Pages:
Workmen's compensation
fully covered
estimates cheerfully given
windows for eight dollars
fire escapes for twenty-five
Benjamin Moore paint the best
but don't forget
Dutch Boy red lead
undercoat first
if you don't mind.

A Requiem

there are so many I miss
so many are gone
a requiem for a world friends my father watched for me
and the family
all at rest blessed I'm sure,
but not here for me.
My words fall on none ears.
My smile is invisible.
 My laughter is in audible. They are ghost ephemeral
Not material but present in memory
and all of the life that we live together
together indelible
etched marked
written and preserved
I am here the past
Worlds and people to be enjoyed
savored like a succulent
fruit cherished,
like an icon celebrated
like a victory now

A Picture at The Prado

Fiery Night, Regulus light pierces Leo's sky
On earth leaves rustle. A lion roars,
Teeth gape from open jaws.

David's son minds his father's flock.
White headed rams and ewes. We watch in horror.

Do we dare to tame the beast?
Do we rather run and hide?
A story is a tale, one as good as any other.
If it works, no matter

Where is truth? God knows.
But is God dead?
That puts de cart before the hearse the darkie said
God a she, God a 'mere' God is philosophy
Is that the point?
Who cares about the answer?

Philosophy is edified or dead,
Both or neither? Deconstructed

There is truth but who knows it?
Philosophers perhaps not dead.

Embedded.

Poem in Progress

My poems
are personal
forged
in the oven
of my discontent
tempered by the fire
of my passion
which burns words
on white paper
like an electric tool
marks wood

and smoke
into the nostrils
perfumes
the page
on which I

the artisan
sets down
my lusts
and rage.

But art abhors
the confessional.
I will use artifice
to engage
my audience,
disguise to veil
the obvious,
guile to create
illusion
as I ply my trade.

Rhyme or Reason

I write a
poem search
for rhyme
and rule
but line
falls flat
I juggle
words
In desperation

Should I stick
to science?
Galileo said
the laws of
shadow making
are the same
on the moon
as on the earth

and apples fall
like planets
said Newton
But I like
Surprises

Hayden Planetarium

Color it dark matter
Dispersed exactly
In the universe
The cosmos poised
Precariously at conception
On a teeter totter

Density is destiny
Miscount six atoms
Per square meter
And the Big Bang ends
In burp or blast
Or whimper

Mass is critical
Cold dark matter
Even if invisible
Gathers up the galaxies
Like love the great
Attractor

Color it dark
Like death
Eros and Thanatos
Frozen in a final
Embrace

Study Group

Freud asked what do
women want Not so wise
a man I thought maybe
he didn't know everything

My students are women groupies
hang on every word and I tell
good jokes besides they think
I know everything.

I dazzle with my erudition\ I
know them better than they
know themselves I bask in
their adoration.

They think I know what
women want and I should
tell Freud
But do I know myself or anything?

Summertime

Last night Leontyne Price
sang "Summertime"
in fire red dress
iridescent
arms outstretched
in benediction

I remember
summer times
Sunset Park
boy hood backyard
watching fire flies
phosphorescent
semaphores
in the dark
I played at war
Caught fire flies
with cupped hands

imprisoned in
empty Ovaltine
cans
and strawberry
jam jars
luminescent
beacons

Fireflies
Were my
imaginary
Armada
Zeros and
Messerschmitts
Dive bombers
Hornets and
Spitfires
Flaming
Incandescent

Last night
Leontyne Price
Sang summertime
arms outstretched
fingers pointing

to the sky
While missile
Streaked over Tel Aviv
flashed
and died

Death

Death shall have no dominion
Dylan said
life is in the livings' court
the heart is on fire
love and desire
needing
wanting
being
up and doing
like McDougall's
animals
we celebrate our senses
sight and smell
listening as well

we laugh at the grim reaper
and go about our way

Eye

can an eye
make its self
can it evolve
incremental changes
natural selection
or does that defy
explanation.
the eye of the bitterly
or the eye of you and I
evolution
or intelligent design
Darwin
or only God
can make an eye
so we can see

Mother's Day

Your day is your
children's day
and your children's day
Is our day
Seamless
Our lives intertwined
Without interruption
A tapestry
Life on a loom
Woven
Together

Turtle

the world sits

on the flat back

of a turtle

and the turtle

sits on the flat back

of another turtle

it is turtles

all the way down

infinite regress

beginning

no ending

paradox

mystery

infinity

a story

without

an end

our world

The End is Near

The end is near
a black hole approaches
arrives in 200 years
life is finite
time is limited
we do not have
a privileged place in the universe
ephemeral
hurling to
our demise
period
or punctuation mark?

at the end
of time

Life

squeeze what you can
out of every moment
treasure every pleasure
enjoy every joy
go down to the sea
lie in the water
come in with the tide
fly on the wings of your imagination
soaring birds

Meaning

meaning matters

wonder of wonder

how does a caterpillar become a buterfly

evolution

or design

how does a sparrow learn to fly

how does a whale learn to dive

how does the summer become the fall

how will the world survive

if the glaciers melt

and the corals die

who is in charge

are we masters of our fate

the clock ticks

the sun sets

and the music stops

Coda

I have had a long life
a happy life
a satisfied life
a productive life
connecting with many
overcoming traumas
an upward trajectory
pleasing
and being pleased
more than I hoped for
more than I ever expected
I will continue
until the clock stops
and the light goes out
I will leave my memoir
and my legacy
for all

Scissors and Paste

Poetry
Cuts up life
Into pieces
And pastes them
On a page

Addendum

Ernie Kafka Sandy Abend Mike Porter Al Sax Leon
Balter Chuck Rothstein Marty Willick

all gone

we miss them very much

they can't hear us

they can't see us

we mourn their loss

but we celebrate our existence

like eating a succulent fruit

or a ripe peach

and listen to the dolphins

singing each to each other

until the lights go out

and the clock stops

for all of us

Photo Section

Introduction to the Photography Section

Like his poetry, the photos of Arnie Richards capture the meaning of a moment in time. With a deceptive simplicity, they leave room for reflection and suggest that we delve deeper into our own reveries. Most of all, a tension between the ordinary and the iconic infuses his photography, asking us to live, explore and devour every moment.

—Janet Lee Bachant, PhD,
psychologist, psychoanalyst,
educator; author of *Exploring the Landscape
of the Mind: An Introduction to Psychodynamic Therapy*

Passing Cuba

On the Beach, Maceio, Brazil

Palm Beach, FL

Urban Sprawl Wuhan, China

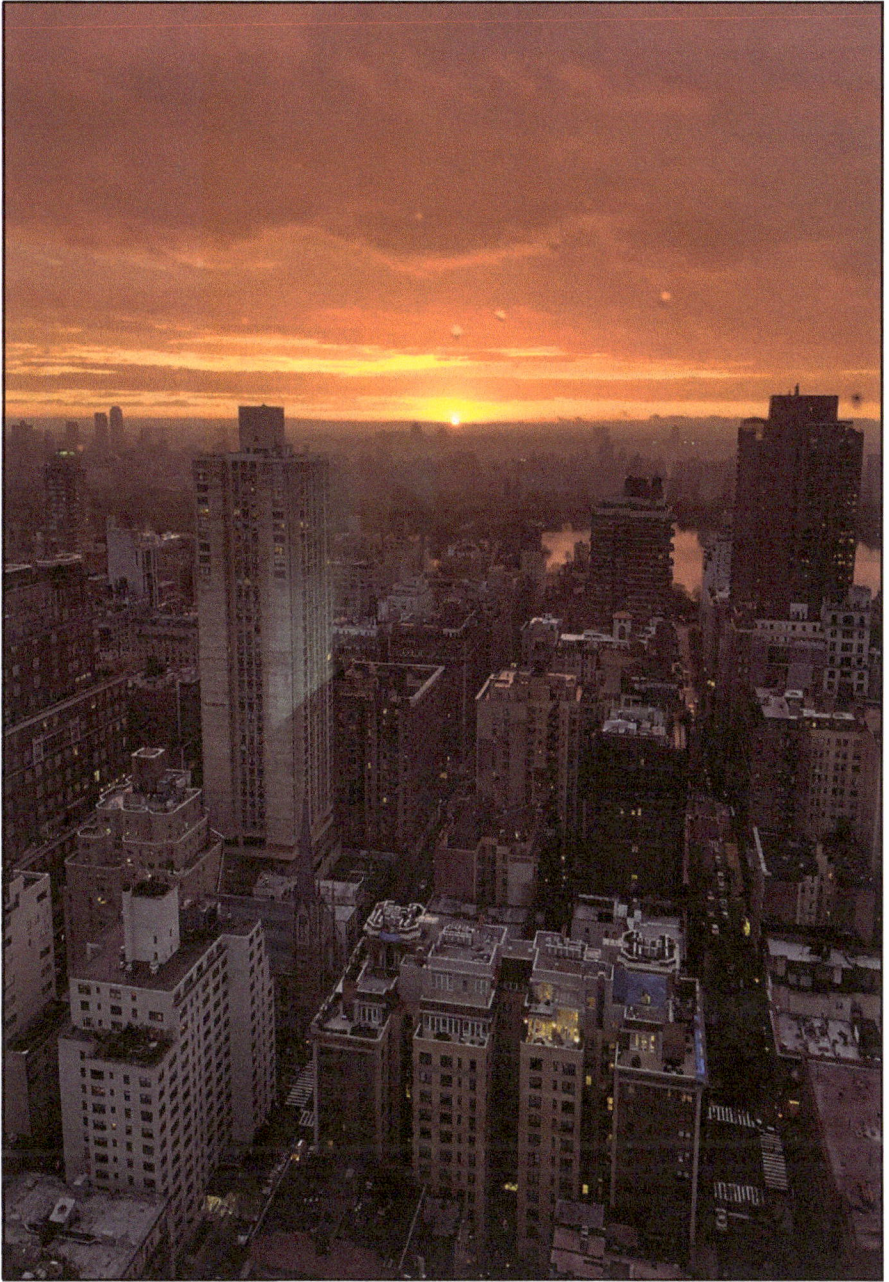
Sunset over New York City

Palm Beach Sunset

Dali Bai

Door of Wuhan Hospital Building

Before the Cruise

Brooklyn Bridge & East River

Drawbridge, Palm Beach, FL

Cityscape & Ferry

Lifeboats

Still Life with Glasses

Beach Umbrellas

At JFK Airport

**Chinese
Boatman**

Water, Wood, & Algae

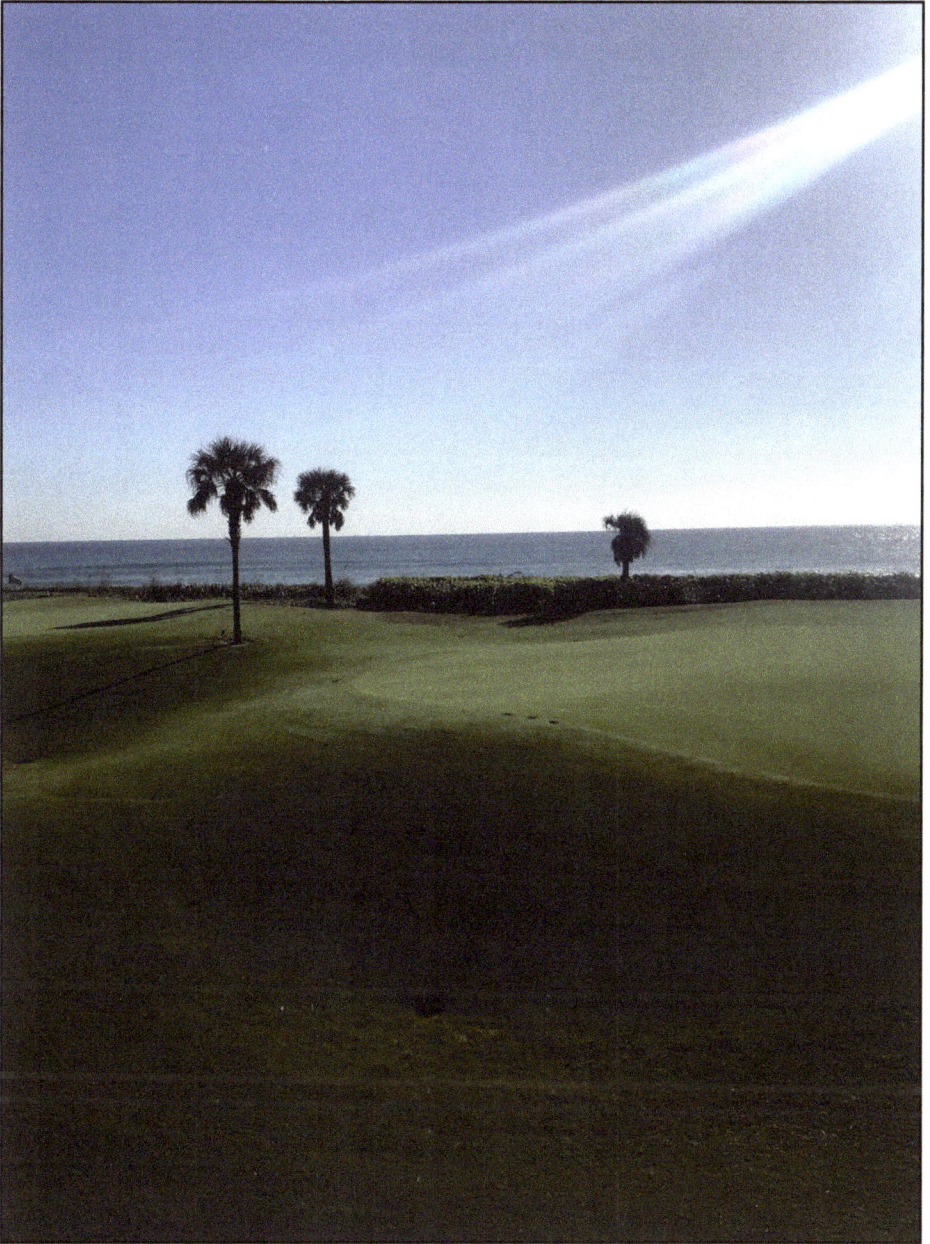

A Hole in One Awaiting a Ball

Houses on a Hill

Rio de Janiero, Favelas

Petra

Windows in the Air

The Four Seasons

Horizon with Palm Trunk

Art & Wheel of Life

Justin as a Toddler

Arlene at Lake Baikal